Offensive Building Blocks

For Basketball

D1722097

Offensive Building Blocks
For Basketball

By Kevin Sivils
All Rights Reserved © 2009 by Kevin Sivils

Published by Kevin Sivils
Printed in the United States of America
KCS Basketball Enterprises, LLC
LGS Publishing

Author: Kevin Sivils

ISBN: 1448630215

EAN-13: 9781448630219

www.kcsbasketball.com

Other Titles by Kevin Sivils:

Game Strategy and Tactics for Basketball:
Bench Coaching for Success

Finding Good Help:
Developing and Utilizing Student Assistant Coaches

Secondary Break Offense:
Maximizing the Running Game

Integrating the Three Point Shot
Into Your Offense

Table of Contents

How to Use This Book

Like many books on offense, this book is filled with Xs and Os. Unlike most books on offense, it is not a compilation of 5-on-5 plays with specific sets or continuities to run. Rather, it is a collection of the components common to most man-to-man offenses and many aspects of attack a zone defense. The building blocks of offense so to speak.

These building blocks are broken down into the 3-on-3 components that make up 5-on-5 offenses. It is extremely rare, and usually the result of an error on the part of the defense, that more than 3 offensive players are involved in the play. Man-to-man offenses are divided into 3-on-3 and 2-on-2 components that when combined make up a 5-on-5 offense. Essentially, what takes place is two different offensive building blocks being executed at the same time, a 3-on-3 building block and a 2-on-2 building block.

The purpose of this book is to present in a clear and logical format the common building blocks used most frequently to create 5-on-5 offenses. These building blocks can be used by the reader to create brand new never before seen offenses! Or, if the reader desires, use them to create the drills necessary to teach an already existing offense using the whole/part or whole/part/whole method of teaching.

Players often do not understand the big picture of 5-on-5 offense and need to learn the 3-on-3 and 2-on-2 building blocks that make up the 5-on-5 offense. By learning the building blocks and how these offensive concepts produce scoring opportunities allows players the means by which to learn to "think" the 5-on-5 game of offensive basketball and "see" the scoring opportunities when they develop.

By no means is every conceivable offensive building block shown and described in this book. Rather it is a comprehensive coverage of the more commonly used offensive building blocks that are widely used.

Offensive Building Blocks

The number of structured offenses and rules based, or free-lance, offenses in the game of basketball are too numerous to count. Regardless of the offense being used, there are a range of basic 3-on-3 and 2-on-2 plays that serve as the building blocks of all offenses, regardless of how the 5-on-5 offense is actually structured, the tempo at which it is played, and the talent available to execute the offense. Teaching these basic building blocks will serve to make the 3-on-3 league games more effective as a learning experience, and by teaching the players "how" to play on offense, the games will be more fun for the players. *Regardless of the offense used, whenever an offensive system breaks down, it is always due to either improper execution of fundamental skills or improper execution of the offensive building block.*

Spacing

Regardless of the style of offense used or the number of players on each team, 5-on-5, 4-on-4, or 3-on-3, spacing is a critical component for the success of the offense. If the players are too close together, it is easy for the defense to defend any option or movement the offense may want to execute. Equally important is the need for the offense to not be spread too far apart, allowing the defense to intercept passes that are too long or making coordination of offensive execution too difficult.

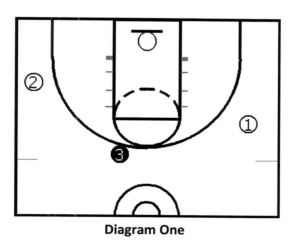

Diagram One

Diagram One shows proper perimeter spacing. The three perimeter players are 15-18 feet apart and behind the three point line. This spacing allows for offensive execution while still spreading the defense out, creating offensive opportunities.

Basket Cut

The basket cut, also known as the "give and go," is one of the most basic offensive plays in basketball and is found in every offense. In the basket cut's simplest form, the player with the ball makes a pass and then cuts to the basket in hopes of receiving the ball back for a lay-up or shot.

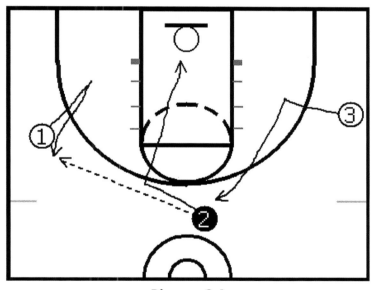

Diagram 2-A

Basket Cut

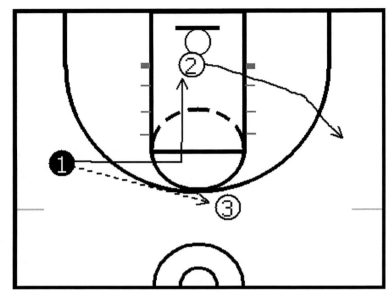

Diagram 2-B

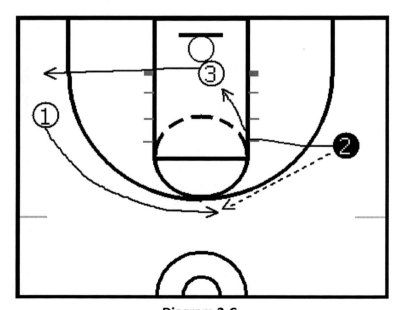

Diagram 2-C

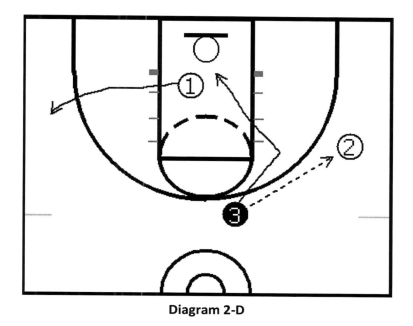

Diagram 2-D

Diagrams 2-A through 2-D all depict examples of a player executing a basket cut. Not only is the player shown basket cutting, but the diagrams show the players moving to fill open spots with correct spacing on the perimeter, beyond the three point line.

The diagrams, in sequence, show how the players reversed the ball from side to side with passes, made basket cuts, and filled the open areas on the perimeter to maintain proper spacing. Important concepts to note are that the basket cutters took their cut all the way to the rim before looking to fill a perimeter spot, the cutters all use a v-cut combined with a change of pace to get open, the ball should be passed away from the defense, and players must face-up in triple threat if they do not have an immediate shot upon receiving the ball.

Replacement Cut

Stationary offensive players are easy to defend, aggressive denial defense can make it extraordinarily difficult to initiate any offensive movement with a pass, and solid on-the-ball pressure defense can make it difficult for the ball handler to re-locate to start the offense. An easy way to initiate some offensive movement is to simply have the perimeter players who are not in possession of the ball execute "replacement cuts." All that this requires is for the players without the ball to make hard v-cuts at least fifteen feet in distance, forcing the aggressive defenders to defend a long distance, making it difficult to prevent the cutter from receiving the ball.

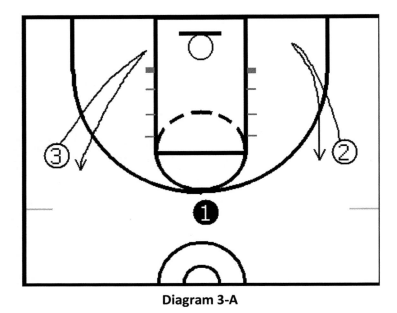

Diagram 3-A

Diagram 3-A depicts the ball as being centered and the two offensive players without the ball moving to get open by making replacement cuts.

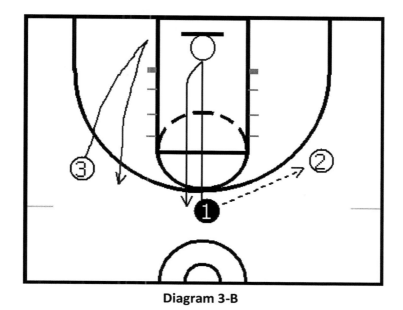

Diagram 3-B

Diagram 3-B depicts the ball on the wing and the two offensive players without the ball making replacement cuts from different angles. Important points are the cutter must travel at least 15-18 feet when making a replacement cut and if not open for an immediate shot upon receiving the ball, the cutter must face-up in triple threat.

Crossing Cut

Crossing cuts allow players to get open, relocate to the correct side of the floor for their position, and force the defense to cover a large area of court. **Diagram 4-A** depicts two perimeters making crossing cuts.

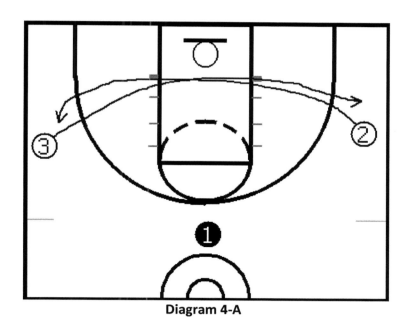

Diagram 4-A

Crossing Cut with Screen

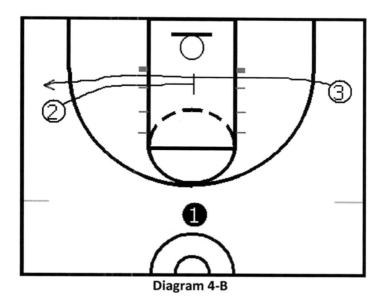

Diagram 4-B

     Diagram 4-B depicts a crossing cut with a screen set by #2 in front of the rim. #3 continues the crossing cut to the other side of the court and spaces out correctly, maintaining 15-18 foot perimeter spacing.

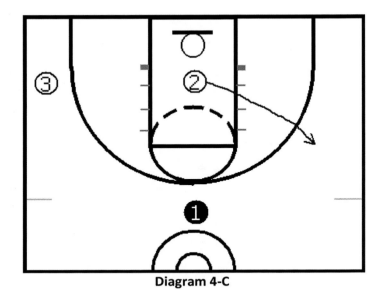

Diagram 4-C

In **Diagram 4-C** #2 continues cutting and spaces out behind the three point line and balances the floor offensively. If a crossing cut with a screen is regularly used, it is wise to designate who the screener will be to avoid confusion and poor execution.

Pass and Screen Away

If the most basic offensive play in basketball is the basket cut, or give and go, then the second most common basic play is the pass and screen away, a cornerstone of motion offense and many other set offenses. In its most basic form, the player with the ball passes to a teammate and then moves in a direction "away" from the ball to set a screen for a teammate who then cuts in the direction of the ball to receive a pass. **Diagrams 5-A through 5-C** depict the pass and screen away concept.

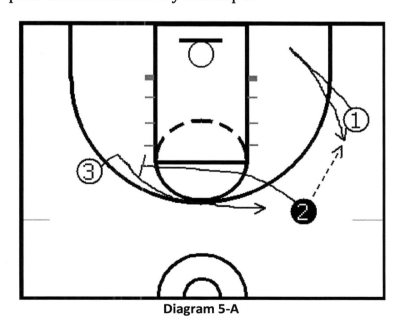

Diagram 5-A

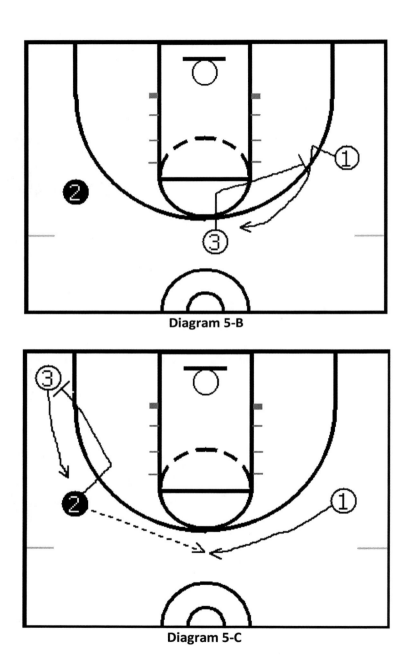

Diagram 5-B

Diagram 5-C

Pass and Flare Screen

The pass and flare screen is a variation of the pass and screen away. It is also an excellent method of setting up a three point shot. In the pass and flare screen, the passer does not set the screen. Instead the screen is set for the passer. **Diagram 6-A** shows how the flare screen is set up. #3 is centered on top and can pass to either side of the court. In **Diagram 6-A**, #3 has passed to #1 on the right side of the

court. #2 makes a v-cut to establish the correct screening angle, screener's back to the corner, and sets a screen on #3's defender, leaving the required one step space for the screen to be legal.

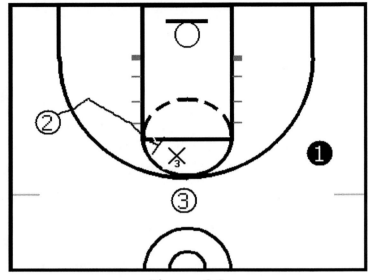

Diagram 6-A

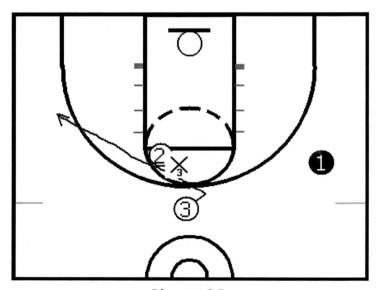

Diagram 6-B

In **Diagram 6-B**, #3 is depicted making a flare cut. To properly execute the flare cut, #3 takes a step towards the ball to draw the defender closer and then executes a v-cut away from the ball. To insure that the defender runs into the flare screen set by #2, #3 rubs shoulders and turns to face the ball while moving to the desired shooting position behind the three point line. #3 should have hands up in a shooting pocket, indicating to #1 exactly where to pass the ball so #3 can shoot quickly.

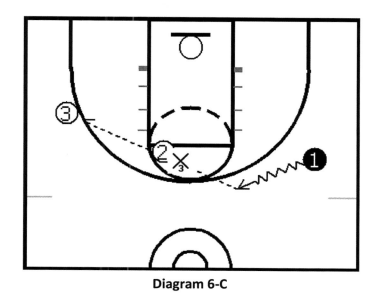

Diagram 6-C

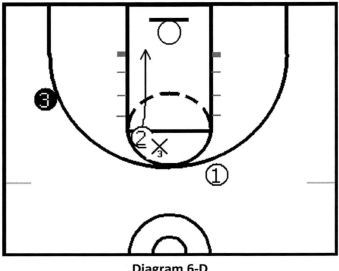

Diagram 6-D

In **Diagram 6-C**, #1 is shown "driving the flare." This means the player on the wing with the ball must "shorten the pass" by taking one or two hard, aggressive dribbles in the direction of the cutter and then executing a crisp two hand overhead pass in which the ball arrives exactly in the shooting pocket of the shooter who has made the flare cut. While the habit of jumping in the air to pass is usually frowned upon and discouraged, driving the flare is one situation in which this is normally bad habit is permissible. Another skill for the passer to consider is to drive the flare, quick stop, and the pass fake away from the flare cutter, freezing the defenders, and then passing the ball to the flare cutter.

Diagram 6-D depicts the screener "slipping the screen" after the pass has been made, cutting to the goal for a possible lay-up. This technique is effective if the defense switches on the flare screen. In this example, #1 was able to complete the pass to #3, but #2's defender switched on the flare screen, preventing #3 from taking an open three point shot. #2 sealed #3's original defender, and then rolled down the lane, giving a hand target, looking for a pass from #3 or an opportunity to post up.

Post Back Screen

Post Back Screen

The post back screen is used to relieve pressure on a perimeter player when the defense uses aggressive denial defense to prevent easy ball movement on the perimeter. It is also a good way for a post player who can shoot from the outside to get open as the post defender must help on the back cut of the perimeter player, leaving the post player open after screening to receive a pass.

Diagram 7 depicts the execution of a post back screen. The low post has stepped away from the post and set a legal back screen, giving the defender one step. The screen must be set with the low post offensive player's back in a direct line with the goal in order for the proper screen angle to be set.

The perimeter player must take a step towards the ball to draw the defender tighter, execute a v-cut directly to the goal, and rub shoulders on the baseline side of the screener. The pass should be a bounce pass directly down the lane line, giving the cutter time to do something with the ball after receiving the pass.

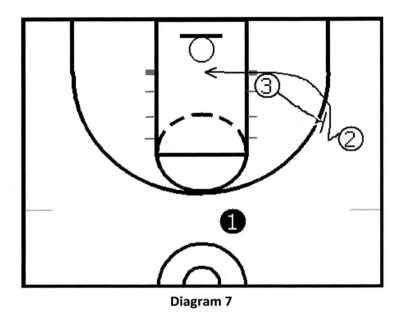

Diagram 7

Post Back Screen/Pin Screen

The use of the post back screen will result in lay-ups in its own right. It is also extremely effective when combined with a pin screen. It is difficult even for an excellent defender to successfully fight through two consecutive screens and deny an offensive player.

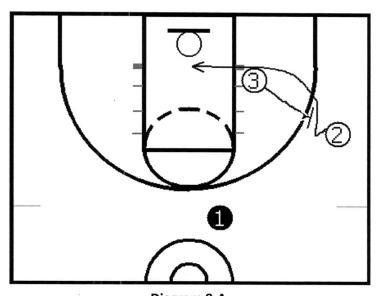

Diagram 8-A

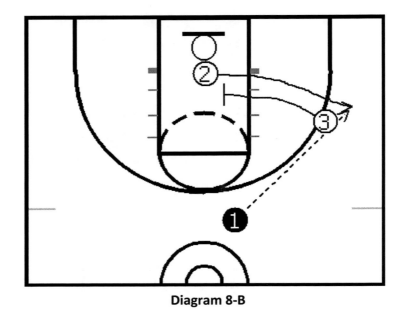

Diagram 8-B

Diagram 8-A depicts again the first half of a back screen/pin screen. **Diagram 8-B** depicts a successful pin screen. The cutter, #2, has made a back cut all the way to the rim. The low post player, #3, has turned and followed #2's defender. #3 sets a screen, pinning #2's defender under the basket. To make the screen even more effective, #3 should execute a rear pivot and post up, sealing #2's defender under the rim and possibly creating an opportunity for the ball to be entered into the low post either from on top or from the wing. #2 executes a pop out cut, rubbing shoulders on #3 when passing, and receives the ball faced up in triple threat at the free throw line extended.

Post Screen Away

The post to post screen away can be one of the most difficult offensive maneuvers for the defense to successfully defend due to the proximity of the cutter to the goal as soon as the cutter comes off the screen. It is also one of the screening situations that most solid defensive

teams spend considerable time working on defending, making it essential that a good

offensive team work on successfully attacking this play.

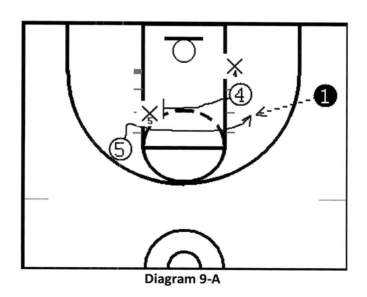

Diagram 9-A

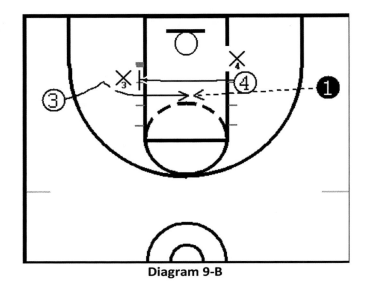

Diagram 9-B

Diagram 9-A depicts a low post to high post opposite screen away. #4 turns, finds #5's defender, makes legal contact with the defender, establishes a low wide base of support, and holds his or her position while #5 executes a v-cut to come off the screen as depicted. #5 must rub shoulders with #4 when coming off the screen and present a hand target and call for the ball.

Note that #5 is not directly opposite from #4 when #4 is occupying the low post. While many offensive teams would position #5 in the opposite low post, by moving #5 up the lane to the high post opposite the ball, the defense is placed in a more difficult position. If #5 was in the low post opposite #4, the defense could simply switch and the low post area would never be open for #5 to receive a pass into the post area. By moving #5 up into the high post opposite the ball, it forces the help side defender higher up the lane, making harder for the defense to simply switch the screen. It also provides a more effective screening angle and cutting angle for a lay-up, making this positioning of offensive post players more effective.

Diagram 9-B depicts a post screen away in which the player being screened for is a perimeter player. In this example, the low post, #4, must turn, find #3's defensive player, and properly execute a screen away. #3 must move into the v-cut slowly, drawing the defender closer allowing #4 to set an legal, effective screen, then accelerate out of the v-cut, presenting a hand target and calling for the ball. It should be noted that the passer must deliver the ball in such a way that it arrives to the receiver as the receiver becomes open, not after the receiver becomes open, allowing the defense to recover.

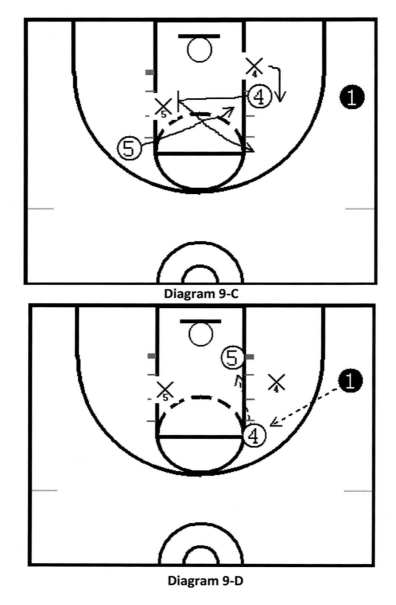

Diagram 9-C

Diagram 9-D

Diagram 9-C depicts a post to post screen with the opposite post positioned in the high post opposite the ball in which the defense has executed a switch. #5 would continue with the normal cut into the lost post area and make contact with the low post defender, sealing the low post defender out for a pass not from the wing, but rather from the ball side high post. **Diagram 9-C** shows #4 executing a rear pivot and sealing the high post opposite defender before flash cutting into the ball side high post. **Diagram 9-D** depicts the entry pass into the high post followed by the high-low pass from #4 to #5 for the score.

UCLA Screen/Cut/Post Feed

The UCLA High Post offense propelled Coach John Wooden's Bruins to 10 NCAA National Championships in 12 years. The first basic building block of the offense is what is now known as the UCLA cut.

Diagram 10-A depicts the offense initiating the UCLA cut by entering the ball on the ball side wing. #1 initiates the pattern by making a v-cut to get open at the free throw line extended beyond the three point line. #2 makes the entry pass to #1 who then faces up to the basket in triple threat. #1 has the immediate offensive options of shooting, driving for a lay-up, or waiting for the play to develop further.

Diagram 10-B shows the high post, #3, stepping out to set a legal back screen for the ball side guard #2 who makes a v-cut to set up the defender for the screen and cuts directly to the basket. If #2 does not receive a pass he or she proceeds to post up on the ball side low post.

UCLA Screen

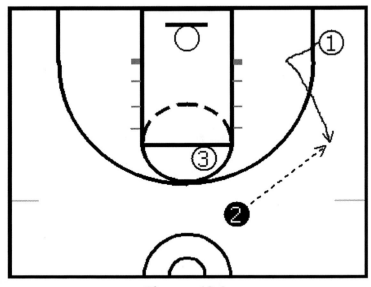

Diagram 10-A

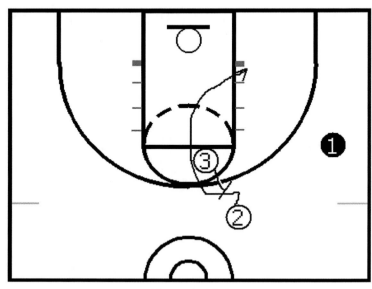

Diagram 10-B

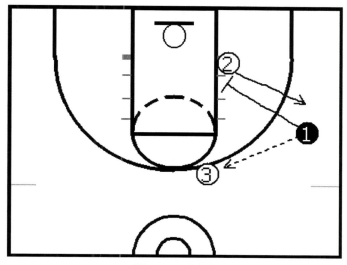

Diagram 10-C

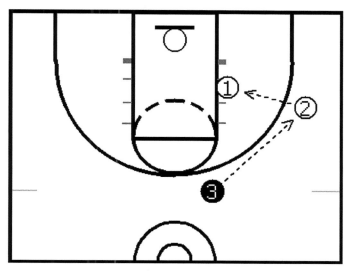

Diagram 10-D

Diagram 10-C depicts the next phase of the UCLA cut. #1 passes the ball to the high post #3 who steps out to receive the ball, relieving any pressure on the ball and if five players were on the court, allowing the offense to execute both a ball side 3-on-3 play and a weak side 2-on-2 play. After passing to #3, #1 sets a down screen for #2 who pops out to the free throw line extended to receive the ball and #1 posts up in the ball side low post.

After receiving the pass from the high post, #2 faces up in triple threat position and looks to either shoot or feed the low post as depicted in **Diagram 10-D**.

Triangle Post

The Chicago Bulls made the Triangle, or Triple Post, Offense famous winning six NBA World Championships. Coach Tex Winter, recognized as the foremost authority on the Triangle, played a huge role in implementing the Triangle with the Bulls, and later with the Los Angeles Lakers who would go on to win a pair of NBA titles with the offense. At the core of the offense is the ball side post feed and cut.

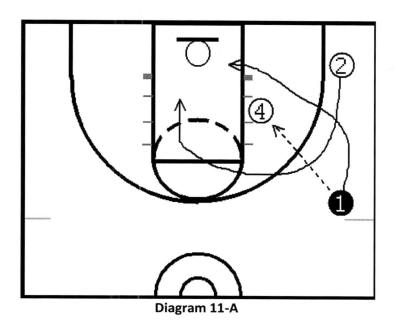

Diagram 11-A

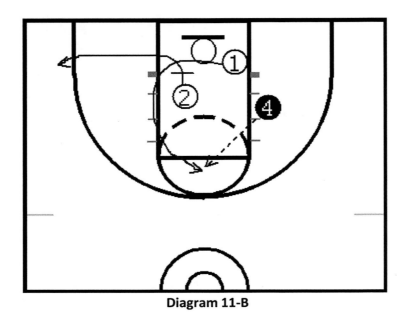

Diagram 11-B

The basic component of the Triangle is a ball side 3-on-3 alignment that consists of a low post who has posted up on what Coach Winter's refers to as the "line of deployment," the line between the ball and the goal, and two perimeter players, one at the free throw line extended area and one in the corner. **Diagram 11-A** depicts this initial alignment and the initial phase of the Triangle cut. #1 (or #2) enters the ball into the low post, #4. The perimeter player who makes the entry pass cuts first, in this case #1 cuts to the baseline side of #4 looking for a return pass for a scoring opportunity. If #1 does not receive a return pass, he or she continues on to the help side low post. #2 is the second cutter and cuts on the high side of the low post, also looking for a pass for a scoring opportunity.

If neither perimeter receives a pass, #2 continues on and sets a downs screen on #1 who cuts towards the foul line area, looking for a pass from #4 as shown in **Diagram 11-B**. After receiving the pass, #1 has four excellent options based on the ball location and the player positioning as shown in **Diagram 11-C**. #1 can shoot a jump shot from the foul line, make a return high low pass to #4, or drive against the grain for a left hand lay-up. The fourth option is to pass to either #2 for a three point shot or making a drop pass to #4, depending on which defensive player rotated to stop #1's drive for a lay-up.

Triangle Post

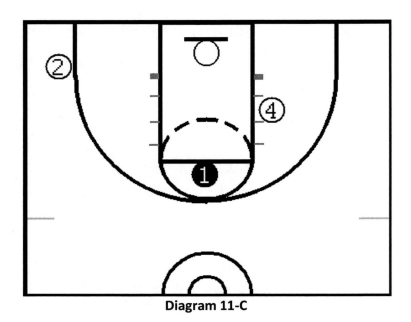

Diagram 11-C

Pinch Post

The second key component of the basic play of the Triangle Offense is the other half of the 5 man unit on the court. The ball side triangle is the 3-on-3 portion of the play. The 2-on-2 portion is initiated on the help side of the floor.

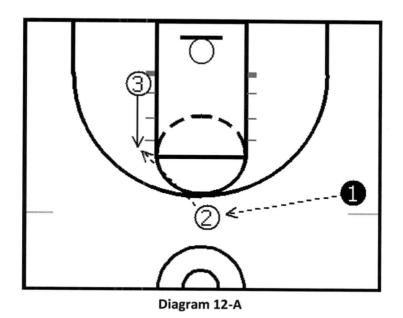

Diagram 12-A

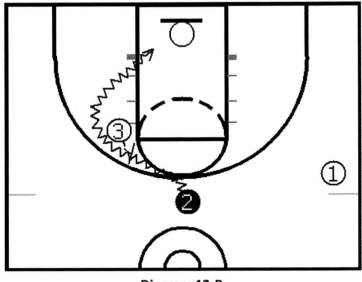

Diagram 12-B

If the ball cannot be entered into the ball side low post it is reversed and the pinch post portion of the play is run. The perimeter spot on top of the key is filled and the ball is passed to the player who fills the spot as shown in **Diagram 12-A**. The help side low post cuts hard into the help side high post, timing the cut so that the low post arrives at the same time as the pass to the player on top does. The post must post up with his or her inside foot forward, sealing the defender on the lane side. The ball can be entered into the pinch post as shown in **Diagram 12-A** or the pinch post can be used to set a ball screen as shown in **Diagram 12-B**.

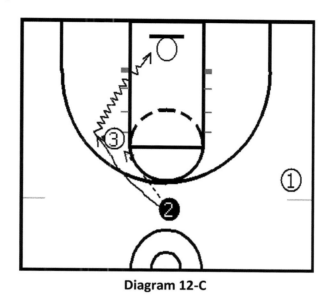

Diagram 12-C

Diagram 12-D

Diagram 12-C shows the perimeter player passing the ball to the pinch post then cutting to the outside of the pinch post, allowing the cutter to use the pinch post as a screen while receiving a handoff at the same time. The perimeter player #2 can then drive to the basket.

Diagram 12-D shows the perimeter player making the cut around the pinch post looking for a return pass from the pinch post. If the cutter does not receive the ball he or she can move the ball side corner or move on to what was the ball side. The pinch post then has the option of driving for a lay-up.

High Post Scissors

Defenses are designed to defend from the inside out, preventing the ball from being entered into the low post and the high post. The high post area is particularly problematic for defenses as so many positive things can happen for the offense when the ball is successfully entered into the high post. **Diagram 13-A** shows just one of many possible ways to occupy the high post area with an offensive player. After getting open in the high post, #3 has received an entry pass from #2.

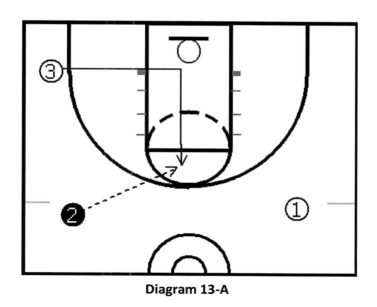

Diagram 13-A

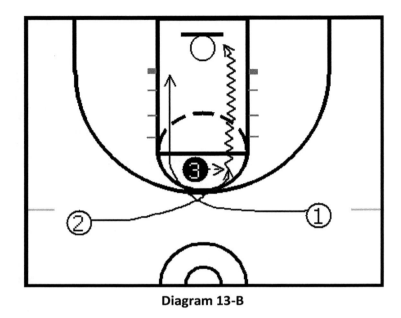

Diagram 13-B

Diagram 13-B depicts the "scissors" cutting action. In this example #1 cuts first, timing the cut with the arrival of the pass to #3. #2 times his or her cut to closely follow that of #1. In this example the defense has lagged behind #2 allowing for a hand-off exchange to take place between #3 and #2. #2 is then able to drive the lane for a lay-up. Note that #1 will be in excellent weak side rebounding position and #3 will be able to cut down the middle of the lane for rebounding position.

Diagram 13-C depicts the completion of the play if a hand-off exchange is not possible. #3 pivots to face the basket in triple threat position and looks to make a lead pass to either #1 or #2 as they cut towards the goal. If a pass for a score is not possible, #3 has the opportunity to play one-on-one against his or her defender.

In a 3-on-3 setting, if a score does not take place, the players should simply continue playing and utilize another offensive building block. In a 5-on-5 setting, the two low post players would set screens for #1 and #2 allowing them to continue on out to the free throw line extended.

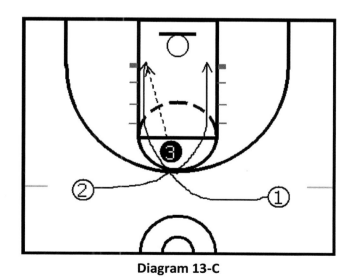

Diagram 13-C

Euro/Double Euro

The Euro, sometimes called an International, is an offensive building block made popular in Europe and has been used successfully in recent times in the United States. Quite simply, a Euro is when a player drives to the goal, drawing the defense to him or her. A teammate fills behind the penetrator, specifically in the area in which the penetrator crossed the three point line. The penetrator executes a quick stop, also referred to as a jump stop, followed by a rear turn or pivot, and passes the ball back to the waiting teammate who has filled in behind. The penetrator turned passer in effect acts as a screener, giving the receiver enough time to take a quality shot.

This simple but effective offensive building block can be seen **in Diagram 14-A.** #1 has penetrated deep into the lane, drawing the defense. #2 fills in directly behind #1, creating an open passing lane.

Euro/Double Euro

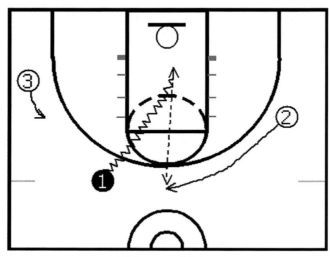

Diagram 14-A

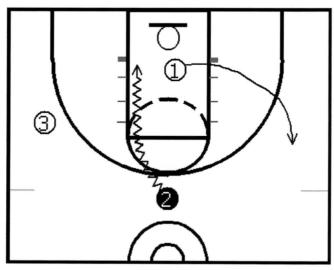

Diagram 14-B

The double Euro is simply a series of Euros executed one after another, **Diagram 14-A** shows the first Euro being executed. The defense does an excellent job of closing out and preventing #2 from having a good shooting opportunity so #2 drives into the lane. #1 balances out the floor by cutting to fill the open side of the court and moving beyond the three point line as shown in **Diagram 14-B**. #3 executes the second half of the Euro by filling in behind #2 and receives the pass from #2 who then balances the court by filling the open area beyond the three point line as shown in **Diagram 14-C**.

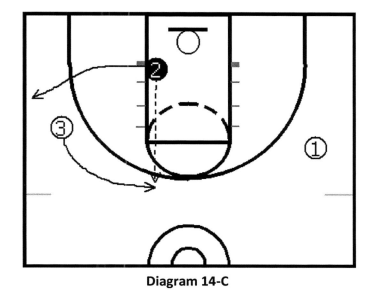

Diagram 14-C

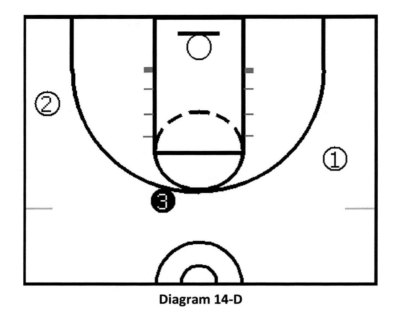

Diagram 14-D

Diagram 14-D depicts the floor after it has been balanced and #3 has received the ball. The three perimeter players have all spaced out beyond the three point line to spread the defense. The offense is now in excellent position to select another offensive building block and continue attacking the defense.

Post Euro

If a team is fortunate enough to have one or more post players who are able to shoot the three point shot, then the post Euro can be added to the list of offensive building blocks in its offensive arsenal. **Diagram 15-A** depicts the first half of a post Euro. #1 drives baseline in this example, drawing the post defender to him or her to stop the dribble penetration. The post play fills in behind the penetrator for a pass as depicted in **Diagram 15-B**. Please note this offensive building block can be used by post players who are not three point shooters but who are effective shooters at the 15 foot range.

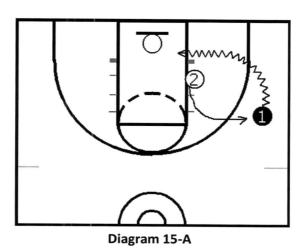

Diagram 15-A

Post Euro

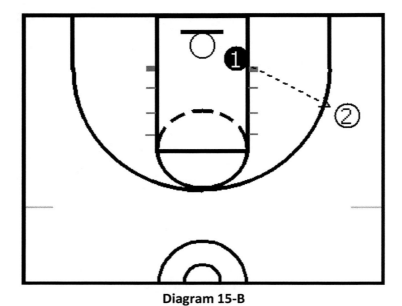

Diagram 15-B

Pick and Roll Wing

Long a staple in the NBA and one of the oldest two player offensive building blocks in the game of basketball, the pick and roll is a relatively simple play that can involve only two offensive players, yet set up an additional, one, two, or even three offensive players for a good shot if proper spacing and alignment is used. After setting the screen, the most important element for the success of any pick and roll type of play is the spacing and alignment of the other three players, or in the case of three-on-three play the other offensive player. Improper spacing and alignment will not only prevent the pick and roll from being successful, but can result in an excellent opportunity for a well trained, aggressive defense to force a turnover.

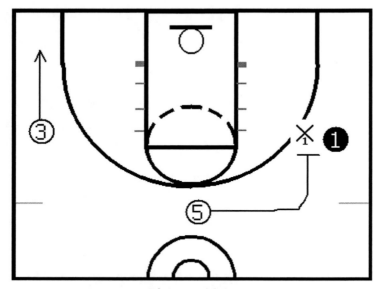

Diagram 16-A

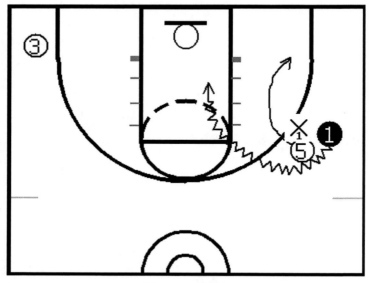

Diagram 16-B

Proper spacing of 15 to 18 feet is depicted in **Diagram 16-A**. #5 approaches the screen angle is such a way that the screen is set perpendicular to #1's defender. #1 has the choice of using the screen or faking the use of the screen and driving in the opposite direction if the defender reacts. ***Note: a poorly set screen is often the result of an improper approach route to the defender, resulting in a screen that is not perpendicular to the defender.***

If #1 uses the on the ball screen set by #5, he or she must drive so close to the screener that contact is made between the two offensive players, ensuring that the defender will get caught on the screen. #1 must take the shortest route possible to the goal, creating the greatest amount of pressure on the defense. **Diagram 16-B** shows how all three players are in now involved in this simple offensive building block. #3 slides to the open area on the baseline for a three point shot. #5 rolls to an open area outside the lane on the side of the floor that the wing pick and roll screen was set. Note, if #5 is a good three point shooter he or she may cut to an area behind the three point line for a possible three point shot.

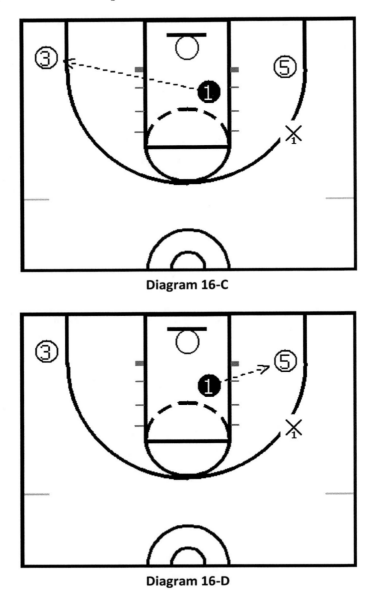

Diagram 16-C

Diagram 16-D

The easiest scoring option is for #1 to simply drive all the way to the goal for a lay-up. It is precisely this scoring option the defense will hope to prevent, and with proper spacing and alignment, the defense's own efforts will create excellent scoring opportunities.

By sliding to the corner as shown in **Diagram 16-C**, #3 is anticipating that his or her defender will be provide help defense to stop the attacking penetration of the ball. When this happens, #1 passes the ball to #3 for an easy, uncontested three point shot, or closer if #3's range is not that far. By sliding down to the

baseline area, #3 makes a successful closeout on defensive recovery more difficult.

In **Diagram 16-D,** #1's penetration has been stopped either by #3's defender or #5's defender and #5 is the player who is open for the undefended shot.

Pick and Roll High

The pick and roll high can be run with a post or perimeter player. The ball handler is centered in the floor when the pick is set. In **Diagram 17-A** #3 has set the on the ball screen and #1 is driving the lane. This simple initial two player building block will set in motion a range of opportunities for the offensive players shown in **Diagram 17-B**. #1 can drive to the goal for a lay-up. #2 is moving to the area behind #1 to set up for a potential Euro. #3 has executed the "roll" portion of the pick and roll and is cutting to the opposite side of the goal. If #1 cannot score a lay-up due to defensive help, he or she has the option of passing to either #3 or #2. **Diagrams 17-C** and **17-D** show the culmination of the possible options of this play.

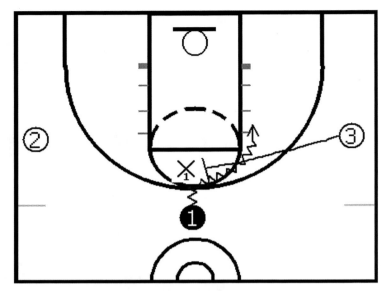

Diagram 17-A

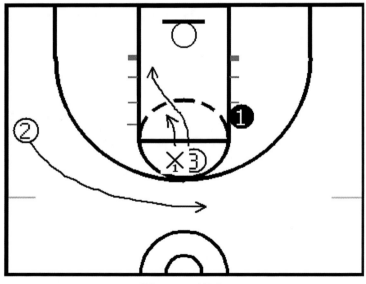

Diagram 17-B

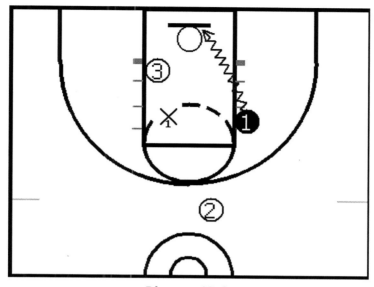

Diagram 17-C

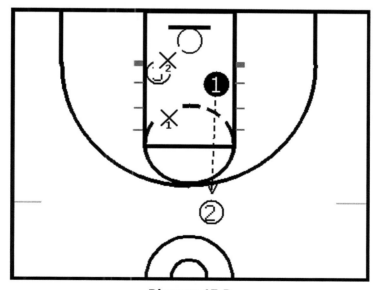

Diagram 17-D

Loop

Aggressive defenses can create havoc for even the most well prepared offensive team. An excellent idea when facing well coached aggressive defensive teams is to use the defense's pressure tactics against the defense in order to enter the offense.

If the defense is using solid guard to wing denial to stop the offense from moving the ball to the free throw line extended area, the perimeter player on top who is in possession of the ball can simply execute a dribble loop by driving the ball to the wing. The perimeter player located at the free throw line extended area makes a shallow cut as shown in **Diagram 18-A**, never turning his or her back to the ball. #2 must make sure that the cut is not too flat or his or her defender may have a trapping opportunity become available simply because #2's cut was too shallow.

The ball can be simply and quickly reversed by pass as this is a difficult offensive cut for #2's defender to cover as shown in **Diagram 18-B**. This simple two player offensive building block is an excellent tool to use to enter the ball into the low post from either the wing area or from on top and can also be used to obtain a three point shot for a perimeter player.

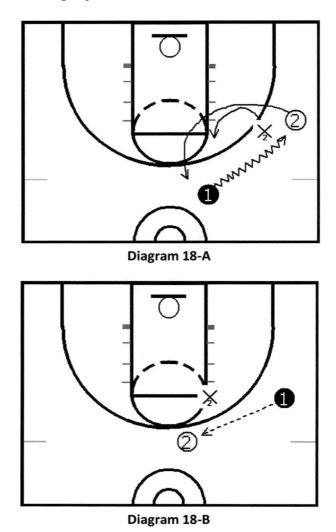

Diagram 18-A

Diagram 18-B

Dribble Follow/Dribble Push

The dribble follow and the dribble push are another simple way to enter the offense against an aggressive defense, move the defenders, or attack a zone. The key to either movement working is for the ball handler to drive at least fifteen feet or more. **Diagram 19-A** shows both a dribble follow and a dribble push being executed. #2 drives fifteen feet in distance, pushing #3 into the corner with the dribble while #1 follows #2, maintaining proper spacing of fifteen to eighteen feet.

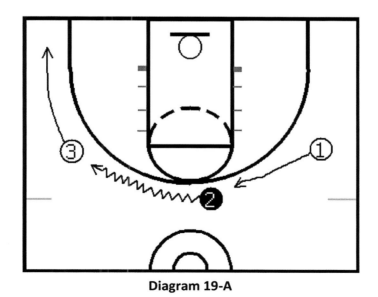

Diagram 19-A

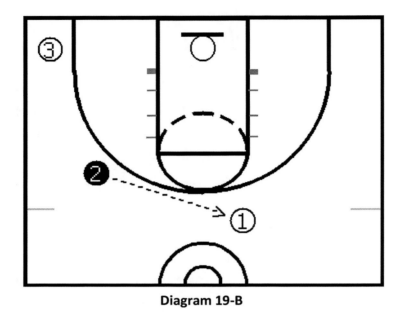

Diagram 19-B

Diagram 19-B shows the ball being reversed to #1 for a possible three point shot or penetration opportunity. This is made easier if #2 makes a hard pass fake to #3 on the baseline to freeze the defense. #1 will usually be open because most defenders will be moving towards a help side defensive position, despite being only one pass away.

Loop Flare

The Loop Flare combines two offensive building blocks into one by combing the dribble loop with the flare screen. This is an excellent way to set up an offensive low post in 5-on-5 play if you have a three point shooter on top as it does not allow the defense to establish help defense behind the offensive low post.

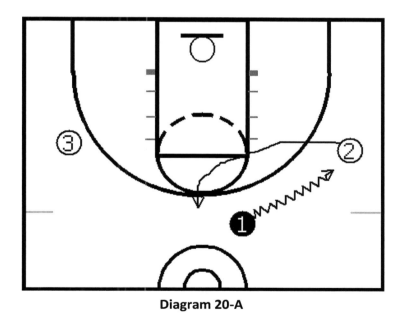

Diagram 20-A

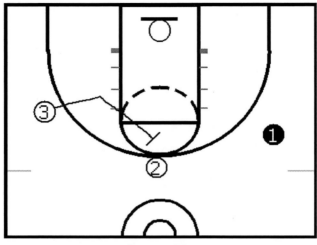

Diagram 20-B

Diagram 20-A shows the dribble loop being executed while **Diagram 20-B** shows #3 setting the flare screen for #2 after the dribble loop has been completed.

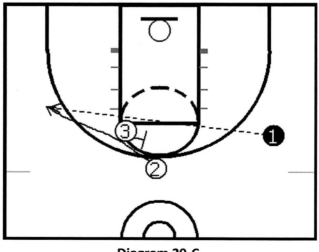

Diagram 20-C

Diagram 20-C shows the flare cut and skip pass being made to set up the three point shot, drive, or post feed if the offensive low post has screened out and cut across the lane (not shown).

Feed the Post

Feeding the post is one of the most essential of all offensive building blocks and should be practiced daily. The key to the success in entering the ball into the offensive low post is successful coordination and communication between the offensive low post player and the perimeter player with ball. Both players must successfully execute a variety of position specific skills such as posting up by the offensive low post and dribbling and passing while under pressure for the perimeter player. Both players must also successfully read how the defense is playing the offensive low post and then coordinate their offensive movements together.

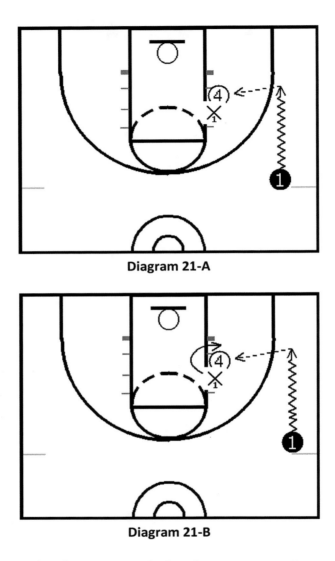

Diagram 21-A

Diagram 21-B

The low post defender, X1, as shown in **Diagram 21-A** is playing on the "high" side of the offensive low post, #4. In order to successfully enter the ball into the offensive low post, #1 must not only recognize how #4 is being defended, but so must #4. To improve the passing angle for the entry pass, #1 must dribble down below the line of deployment and pass the ball to #4 but away from the defender X1. #4 must hold his or her seal until after receiving the ball from #1. After passing to the offensive low post, #1 must execute a tactic known as feeding the post and moving.

Diagram 21-B shows an active low post defender who has shifted his or her defensive position from the high side of the offensive low post #4 to the low side while #1 was dribbling down to improve the passing angle for the entry pass to the offensive low post. The ball can still be safely entered into the offensive low post by passing the ball to the high side of the offensive low post player and once again, away from the defender.

The offensive low post player can either score after receiving the entry pass or make one of many passes that can lead to a scoring opportunity for a teammate.

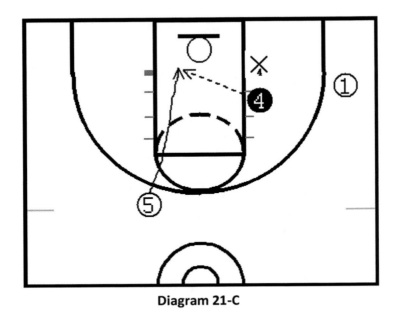

Diagram 21-C

Diagram 21-C depicts the post to post pass as the high post opposite, #5 cuts down the other side of the lane. By positioning the other post player in the high post area opposite the offensive low post, if the defense makes the decision to double team the offensive low post with the other post defender, it leaves the defense vulnerable to the "back half" cut resulting in an easy lay-up for the offense.

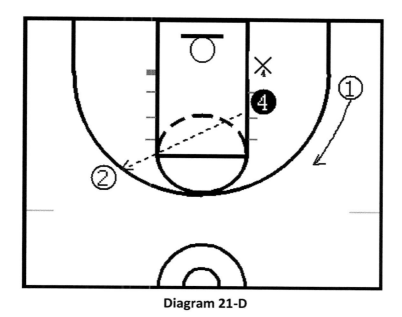

Diagram 21-D

Another excellent scoring opportunity that punishes the defense for double teaming the offensive low post with a help defender is the fan pass diagonal as shown in **Diagram 21-D.** #4 squares his or her shoulders to the perimeter player whose defender has double teamed the low post. That perimeter player must move to the area diagonally opposite the offensive low post as shown in **Diagram 21-D**. Another pass for a score option would be for #4 to pass the ball to #1 who has feed the post and moved, possible leaving his or her defensive player behind. This last tactic is effective against teams that double team offensive low post off the perimeter instead of from the help side.

Penetrate and Pitch

The two man offensive building block known as penetrate and pitch has been around since the early days of basketball. The addition of the three point line to the game has made this basic play even more important for a team to have it included somewhere in its offense.

Diagram 22 shows this simple play in which #1 has penetrated into the lane forcing #2's defender to give help in order to prevent the easy lay-up. This creates a passing lane for #1 to make a pass for a score to #2. In addition to simply setting up the three point shot, the penetrate and pitch sets up multiple opportunities to break down an aggressive defense that recovers well by using the individual recovering defender's forward momentum against him or her and "driving against the grain." This tactic allows the offensive player to use the hustle of the defender against him or herself.

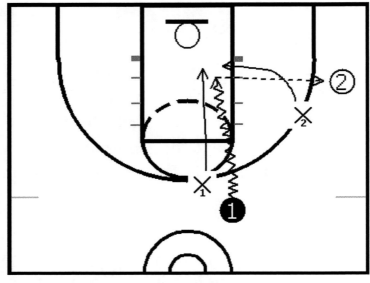

Diagram 22

Penetrate and Skip

Penetrate and skip is a variation of penetrate and pitch. In **Diagram 23** #1 drives the lane from the wing area, drawing #2's defender creating the skip pass to #2.

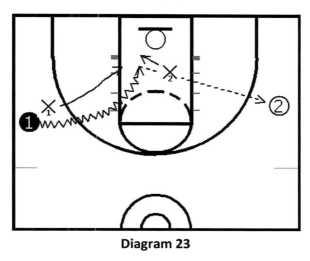

Diagram 23

Baseline Drift

The baseline drift and the I-cut are a pair of simple two player offensive building blocks that can be executed independently or together. **Diagram 24** shows the baseline drift pass being executed as well as an I-cut by the ball side offensive low post player. #2 drives baseline in an attempt to draw defenders. #1 recognizes the play and "drifts" to the baseline and spots up for a three point shot attempt. #3 executes a rear turn and takes a large step back and into the lane, spotting up for a short post shot in front of the goal. The drift pass should be thrown behind the backboard to avoid any defensive players from tipping the ball.

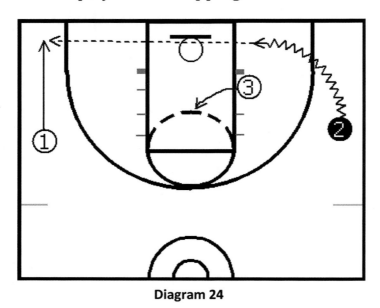

Diagram 24

I-Cut

The I-cut pass is made by throwing a hook pass over the defenders to the waiting post player. The post player makes a rear turn, sealing any defender rotating to him or her on his backside. The post player then steps o the area in front of the rim. This is an unnatural move for the defense to cover. This is demonstrated in **Diagram 25**.

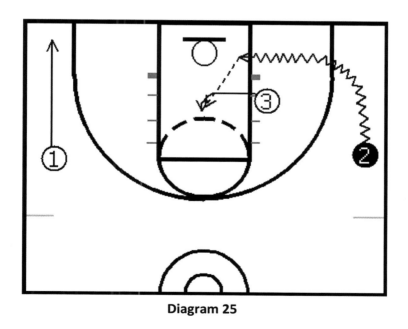

Diagram 25

Backdoor Cut

Coach Pete Carrill at Princeton University almost single-handedly brought back the idea of the backdoor cut with his success at Princeton University running an offense that relied heavily on backdoor cutting action. The back cut, also known as the backdoor cut, is an excellent weapon to use against teams that play an aggressive denial or pressure defense. The intent of the back cut is to use the defender's own aggressive play and positioning against him or her.

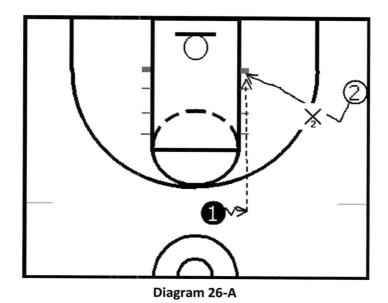

Diagram 26-A

Diagram 26-A shows the most basic and common of back cuts with #1 in possession of the ball on the top of the lane area and X2 is denying #2. #2 starts to break towards the ball which forces X2 to deny more aggressively. #2 then accelerates after v-cutting (a change of direction must always be accompanied by a change of pace) and cutting behind the defender and directly towards the goal. #1 must drive the ball to be in a position to throw a bounce pass directly down the lane line. This type of pass is the most difficult for the recovering defender to deflect and by passing directly down the lane line gives #2 an easier pass to catch and room to maneuver to score after receiving the pass.

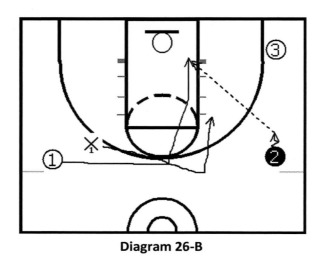

Diagram 26-B

Diagram 26-B depicts a back cut from another, less common angle of attack. The principles of execution are the same with the exception of the pass down the lane line.

Skip Pass & Drive Baseline

Strong defensive teams will always position players in some form of help defense to allow for more disruptive pressure to be applied to the ball and to deny key offensive areas of the court such as the offensive low post. The skip pass is an excellent offensive weapon against such types of defense for two reasons. The defense must make a quick change from one side of the court to the other, creating opportunities for mistakes in defensive positioning. The defense may also closeout too tightly on the offensive player with the ball, creating an opportunity for dribble penetration. **Diagram 27-A** shows a simple skip pass which can be all that is needed to obtain an open three point shot.

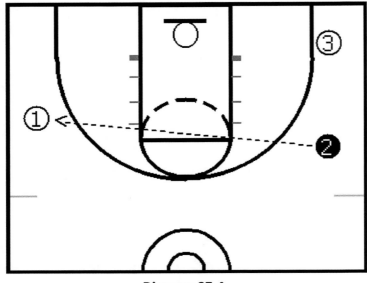

Diagram 27-A

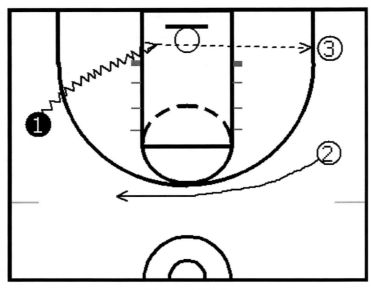

Diagram 27-B

Diagram 27-B shows a skip pass and baseline drive. #1 has received the skip pass and an opportunity to drive baseline has been created. The help defender who is also responsible for #3 must give help to stop the penetration, leaving #3 open for a pass.

Skip Pass & Drive Middle

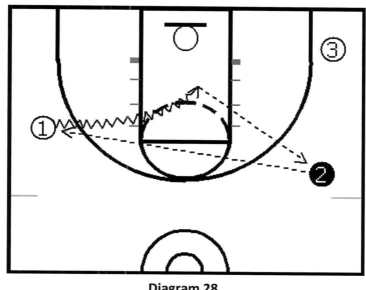

Diagram 28

The skip pass and drive middle is another variation of penetration off a skip pass. After #1 receives the skip pass from #2, #1 executes an up fake and drives middle drawing #2's

defensive player. #2 should be spotting up for a three point shot and showing #1 a triple threat stance with a shooting pocket indicating he or she is open and ready to shoot upon receiving the ball. This simple offensive building block is shown in **Diagram 28**.

Skip Pass & Drive Middle with Back Cut

This offensive building block involves simple but uncomplicated timing. As shown in **Diagram 29-A**, #2 makes the skip pass to #1 who then up fakes and drives the middle. #2 then spots up for a three point shot and shows a shooting pocket to hold the attention and position of his or her defender. #1 drives the middle as shown in **Diagram 29-B.**

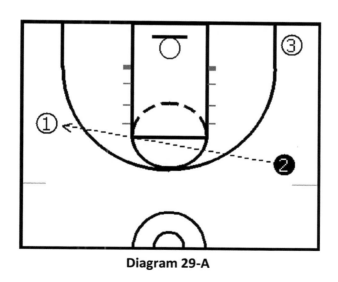

Diagram 29-A

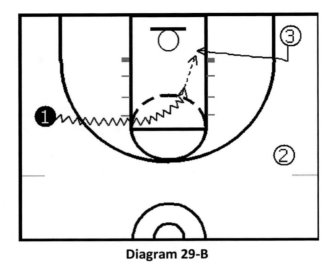

Diagram 29-B

By #2 holding his or her defender, this forces #3's defender to make a choice of staying with #3 or stopping the penetration by #1. #3 makes a v-cut as shown in **Diagram 30-B**

behind his or her defender and receives a backdoor pass from #1. The timing of this cut takes practice but is easy to learn. The key is for #3 to watch his or her defender's head. When the defender takes a quick glance at the penetrator, #3 executes the v-cut.

Dribble Exchange

The dribble exchange, or hand-off, harkens back to the early days of the game of basketball and this basic two player offensive building block is starting to make a comeback. Essentially, the play is a pick and roll in which the ball handler is setting the pick and the other player takes the ball in an exchange or hand-off and then drives in the desired direction.

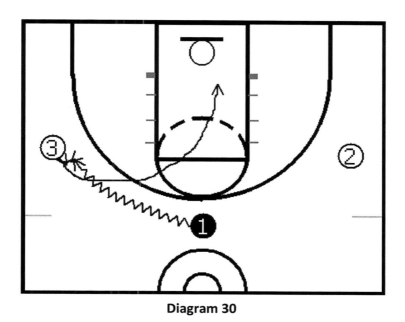

Diagram 30

Diagram 30 depicts this simple two player concept. It can be incorporated into a multi-player play, be combined with a continuous series of dribble exchanges, or simply be a standalone play. In **Diagram 30**, #3 is driving down the lane for a lay-up. #2 has spaced correctly and if the defense is able to stop #3's penetration, #2 has several options which include a Euro or setting up a penetrate and pitch with #3.

2-on-2 Offensive Building Blocks

Many of the building blocks in this part of the book have already been demonstrated as part of a 3-on-3 building block. They are shown here again for more clarity and to provide the reader with a more clear depiction of the 2-on-2 component of the 3-on-3 building block.

Give and Go

The most basic two player offensive play (building block) in the game of basketball is the give and go. Almost every offensive building block incorporates some aspect of this basic play.

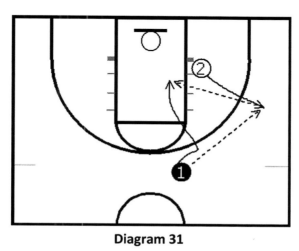

Diagram 31

Diagram 31 depicts the give and go with #2 cutting to get open to receive a pass from #1. After passing to #2, who immediately faces up in triple threat position facing the basket and looking under the net, #1 takes a step towards the ball and then v-cuts and accelerates towards the basket, looking for a return pass from #2. #1 should provide #2 with a target hand to pass to so #2 will throw a leading pass to #1. The pass should be made with sufficient court space for #1 to shoot a lay-up.

Diagram 32 depicts a give and go from a different area on the court. Instead of the common guard/forward pass that is the most frequently used form of the give and go, **Diagram 32** depicts a give and go from a guard to guard pass.

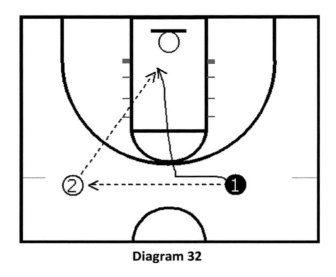

Diagram 32

Dribble Loop

The dribble loop is an excellent way to enter the ball to the wing area against a tough defense that plays excellent denial when one pass away from the ball. **Diagram 33-A** depicts the dribble portion of the loop. #1 dribbles at #2 who makes a shallow, looping cut to the area vacated by #1. #2 must never turn his or her back to the ball and should face-up ready to receive a pass for a post feed or a shot as soon as #2 is in position to face the basket.

In **Diagram 33-B** #1 rips the ball across his or her chest and passes the ball away from

both the on ball defender and #2's defender, using the outside hand to make the pass.

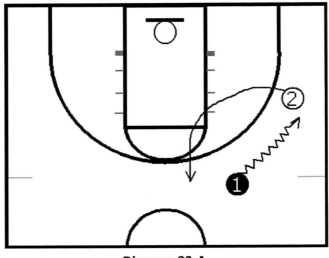

Diagram 33-A

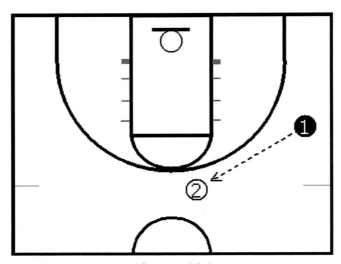

Diagram 33-B

Backdoor Cut

The backdoor cut is a basic variation of the give and go play and is utilized when the defense is successfully denying a direct pass between two players. A guard to forward backdoor pass is shown in **Diagram 34**. Note that #2 does not make a direct cut but steps towards the ball to set the defender up and then makes a v-cut complete with acceleration out of the v-cut and providing a hand target for the passer, #1. #1 reads that #2 is going to execute a backdoor cut (the use of a clenched fist by #2 is an excellent silent signal to indicate that a backdoor cut is about to be made) and drives to the lane line and makes a bounce pass directly down the lane line to #2. This ensures that #2 will know where the ball will be passed and provide enough space to shoot a lay-up after catching the ball. It also lessens the likelihood that the pass will be intercepted by a help side defender stepping to the pass.

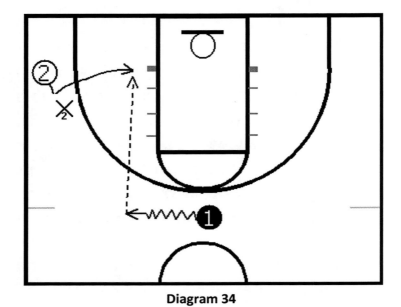

Diagram 34

Pinch Post Series

The popularity of the Triangle Offense, utilized by the NBA World Champions Chicago Bulls and Los Angeles Lakers, has shown astute basketball coaches and fans alike the utility of the "pinch post" play. **Diagram 35-A** depicts the ball being entered into the pinch post area. #2 should have his or her inside foot forward and provide the passer with a hand target away from the defense.

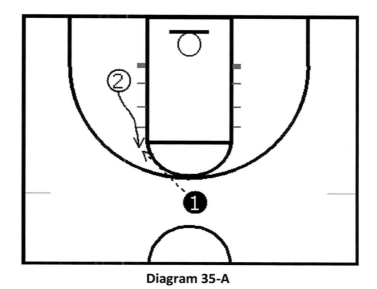

Diagram 35-A

Diagram 35-B shows the hand-off option. After passing the ball into the pinch post, the passer makes a hard cut tight to the post and takes a hand-off from the pinch post. A variety of the options now present themselves, including using the pinch post as a ball screen to drive the middle of the lane as shown in **Diagram 35-C**.

Diagram 35-D depicts using the hand-off option to execute a dribble down to feed the low post. After handing off the ball to the perimeter player, the pinch post rolls down the lane, sealing out his or her defender and establishing a low post position.

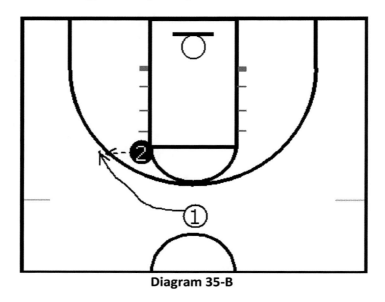

Diagram 35-B

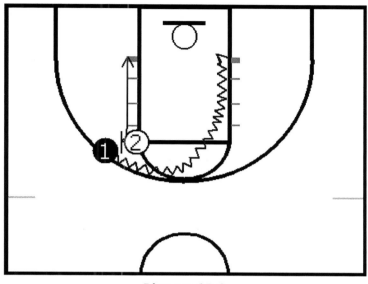

Diagram 35-C

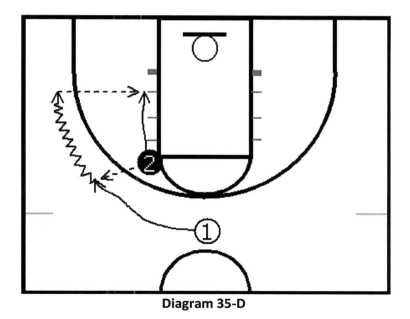

Diagram 35-D

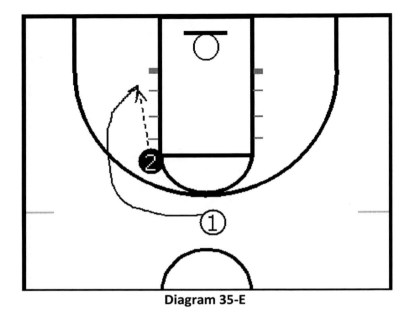

Diagram 35-E

    Diagram 35-E depicts the "around" option of the pinch post series. #1 cuts around the pinch post #2 and looks to receive a return pass for a lay-up. #2 should fake the hand-off and then turn aggressively towards the lane and face-up to the basket.

Penetrate and Pass

Using the dribble drive to create openings for a teammate has long been a staple of offensive basketball. The basic concept is to dribble penetrate and draw a defender away from an offensive player, thereby creating a scoring opportunity. **Diagram 36-A** depicts the draw and kick play. #2 turns the corner on his or her defender and drives the lane, "drawing" the defender from #1, and then "kicking" the ball to #1 for a shot or drive. **Diagram 36-B** shows the "penetrate and skip" play. #1 penetrates into the lane from the wing drawing or freezing #2's defender and then making a skip pass.

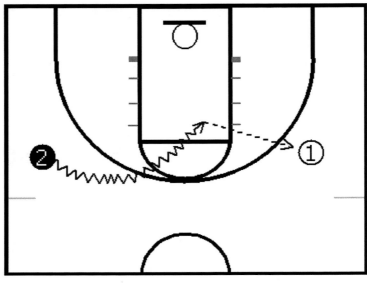

Diagram 36-A

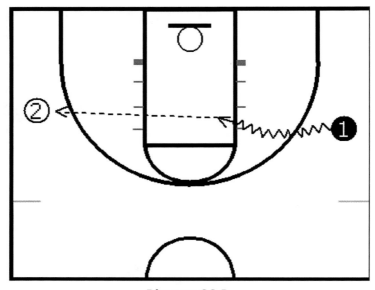

Diagram 36-B

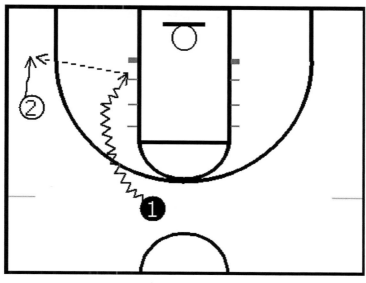

Diagram 36-C

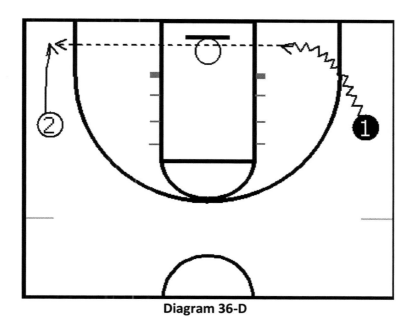

Diagram 36-D

Diagram 36-C shows the "penetrate and pitch" concept. #1 drives down the lane line or penetrates the lane, drawing #2's defender and then "pitches" the ball to #2 for a shot or drive. **Diagram 36-D** shows the "baseline drift" play. #1 drives baseline. #2 recognizes the opportunity and "drifts" to the corner on the baseline. If #1 is able to draw #2's defender, a pass made behind the backboard is open and a 3 pt. shot for #2 can be obtained.

About the author: A 24 year veteran of the coaching profession, with twenty-two of those years spent as a varsity head coach, Coach Kevin Sivils amassed 464 wins and his teams earned berths in the state play-offs 19 out of 22 seasons with his teams advancing to the state semi-finals three times. An eight time Coach of the Year Award winner, Coach Sivils has traveled as far as the Central African Republic to conduct coaching clinics. Coach Sivils first coaching stint was as an assistant coach for his college alma mater, Greenville College, located in Greenville, Illinois.

Coach Sivils holds a BA with a major in physical education and a minor in social studies from Greenville College and a MS in Kinesiology with a specialization in Sport Psychology from Louisiana State University. He also holds a Sport Management certification from the United States Sports Academy.

In addition to being a basketball coach, Coach Sivils is a classroom instructor and has taught U.S. Government, U.S. History, the History of WW II, and Physical Education. He has served as an Athletic Director and Assistant Athletic Director over the years of his career and has also been involved in numerous professional athletic organizations.

Sivils is married to the former Lisa Green of Jackson, Michigan, and the happy couple are the proud parents of three children, Danny, Katie, and Emily. Rounding out the Sivils family are three dogs, Angel, Berkeley, and Al. A native of Louisiana, Coach Sivils currently resides in the Great State of Texas.

For more information on books, coaching clinics, and coaching newsletter please visit our web site at:

www.kcsbasketball.com

- or —

Contact Coach Sivils by e-mail at:

info@kcsbasketball.com